Business Synergy Unmasked

The Smart Entrepreneur's Guide to Exploiting the Power of Business Synergy

By

Noman Shams

Table of Contents

Introduction...1

Chapter 1 5

What is Synergy?...5

The Two Types of Synergy That Matter 8

Internal Synergy..9

External Synergy 10

Chapter 2...12

Benefits of Business Synergy 12

Advantages of Business Synergy...............................12

Chapter 3...17

How to Create Profitable Business Synergies 17

Your Business Model and Business Strategy 18

Know Your Marketing Audience Inside-out 19

Thinking Collaboration over Competition...................21

The Dream 100 22

How to Establish Your Dream 100...........................23

Who are the established thought leaders that my potential customers follow, buy their products, or consume their content? 23

Chapter 4...26

Modern Ways Small Businesses and Entrepreneurs Build Profitable Synergies..26

#1. Affiliate Marketing 26

#2. Joint Ventures 27

#3. Task Outsourcing 28

Conclusion 30

Introduction

Every entrepreneur sets out to solve a problem or series of identified problems in society and then grow a profitable business.

Growth is the most important aspect of a business's life cycle; without it, no business succeeds and every entrepreneur would just turn out a failure.

Growth means many things to many entrepreneurs and businesses.

It can mean making more sales, generating more revenue, creating more product lines, expanding to new locations, getting more funding in the case of startups, increasing capacity by hiring and so much more.

Among the many things that make up growth for a business, generating more sales and making more money is at the forefront of it.

Without more revenue, no business would become self-sustaining, and business death would become an eventuality.

This is why marketing is the most important thing every business needs to succeed in to grow…

According to the US Chamber of Commerce… <u>8 out of every 10 small business close within the first 5 years of establishment.</u>

Why is this shocking statistic possible?

I will tell you.

It's obviously because of the lack of sales and generation of revenue to power the growth of the business.

And how do they generate revenues?

By having a continuous inflow of customers to serve, who pay them…
And how do they get a steady inflow of customers?

By marketing continuously and driving in new prospects through brand awareness and other marketing campaign objectives.

Research shows that businesses that master the art of marketing early enough in their life cycle, experience massive growth than those that do not.

Apple Inc. succeeded not because they created wonderful and innovative products from the beginning but because Steve Jobs was a wonder at marketing their creations and getting them into as many offices and homes as possible.

So, as an entrepreneur, if you want to succeed with your venture or business, you must focus on marketing to grow your business and become profitable…

Business synergy is one of the often overlooked and fastest methods to implement marketing and grow exponentially.
The problem is that many entrepreneurs do not necessarily pay attention to business synergy or understand it from the perspective from which they can see how powerful synergy is to the growth of their business.

But that's about to change.

In this book, I want to help as many entrepreneurs as are reading this book to lift the blindfold from their eyes and get them to see the new light of synergy in the core areas of their businesses, where they can implement it and quickly grow and become profitable.

Synergy is not just for big corporations with deep pockets, large teams, and sophisticated strategies that make them able to make industry shaking synergistic moves.

We are going to explore synergy at the microlevel… The level where it even matters more for small businesses and entrepreneurs like you. Let's begin!

Chapter 1

What is Synergy?

Synergy is one of the prominent corporate buzzwords that you hear often and begin to get confused about, especially if you are just a small business owner.

In this book, I aim to demystify business synergy and bring it down to the level where your knowledge of synergy can help you ignite a lightbulb in your head and make you begin to see the massive ways you can take advantage of business synergy to propel your business in sales, profits, and growth.

I am going to show you how savvy entrepreneurs like you have used simple synergistic steps to take their businesses from $0 to millions of dollars in sales simply by mastering the power of synergy.

Now, what does everyone understand as synergy?

> *"Synergy is a mutually advantageous conjunction or compatibility of distinct business participants or elements such as resources or efforts."*
> **(Merriam-Webster dictionary)**

By this definition, we can see that synergy simply involves pooling resources together or coming together to achieve a common goal.

When two persons or entities work together to achieve a common goal, that's synergy.

In the corporate world, synergy is often broadly defined and incorporated into the overall company growth strategy.

You hear things like acquisitions, mergers, franchising, new product developments and so much more.

This is the way big Silicon Valley corporations like Google, Facebook, and Microsoft Corporations have been growing and dipping their massive corporate feet into new industries.

For example, according to the <u>New York Times Deal book</u>, Google was acquiring more than one company a week between 2010 and 2011.

These acquisitions allowed Google to use the power of synergy to grow and expand exponentially into new sub-sectors of the ICT industry as well as grow in product portfolio.

These acquisitions were deals worth multiple billions of dollars. This is not the kind of corporate business synergy I want to reveal to you in this book.

The Google kind of synergy and growth will only make sense to you if you are an investor holding Alphabet Inc shares, the parent company of Google.

As an entrepreneur or small business owner looking to generate more revenue and grow your business…

The next type of synergy, which is often overlooked and not talked about is what I am going to reveal to you, and it is what will help you push your business to massive growth and profitability.

But first, let's talk about the two types of synergy you should be paying attention to.

The Two Types of Synergy That Matter

Every business exists in two environments, the internal and external environments; as an entrepreneur, the synergy you create for your business will depend on the factors in these two environments that you pay attention to and deem as important.

> *"Business environment means a collection of individuals, entities and other factors, which may or may not be under the control of an organization but can affect its performance, profitability, growth, and survival."*
> **(businessjargons.com)**

The concept of business environment is very important to business growth and is the framework upon which beneficial business synergies are formed.

There are two types of business environments, the internal business environment, and the external business environment.

The internal business environment includes your team, your core values, your objectives, your business goals, your tools and resources, your operations, and your business model among others...

Internal Synergy

Without internal synergy among all the elements that make up your internal business environment, your business will not experience growth.

Internal synergy exists when the different units that make your business work together to achieve your business goals and objectives with the resources available.

For example, if your marketing team is great at generating and pumping in new leads into your business; is the sales team equally great at closing them and getting the sale?

If both teams work together to form a solid synergy, then you'd be pretty confident that your business will experience growth because your marketing budget is getting well-spent and bringing in more sales and more new customers.

External Synergy

External synergy is built through a careful study of the external business environment to identify profitable opportunities and avoidable threats.

As a business owner or entrepreneur, you don't have much control over the external business environment, but you can hold a close lens over it to pick out synergistic opportunities to exploit.

The external environment is huge and varied, and there are many players in there.

The external environment includes customers, competitors, suppliers, target audience (market), government policies, and laws, technology, and so much more.

Your job as a growth-inclined entrepreneur is to seek out opportunities in this red ocean of the external environment and carve out profitable opportunities for synergy and then pursue it with all determination.

You can only see these opportunities by focusing on what matters for your business and filtering out every other noise and distraction…

For any new business, what matters is generating revenue, and you can only do this by creating a blue ocean for your brand and products.

In the next few chapters, we will dive in and talk about how you can achieve this using synergy.

Chapter 2

Benefits of Business Synergy

Before we dive in on the tactics you can use to rapidly build synergy for your small business and experience exponential growth, let's briefly talk about the massive benefits and advantages synergy offers you.

Advantages of Business Synergy

Faster Results

One of the biggest benefits your business is going to experience with synergy is the rapid implementation of business goals and achievement of faster results, this is especially if you can maintain an ecosystem of synergy within your business's internal environment.

The synergy between the different units of your workforce means that information, communication, and data processing and transfer become much more efficient, and key decision making faster.

In a business ecosystem where synergy exists between the different business functions, everyone knows what needs to be done and does it.

This concerted effort aggregates to become the driving force that keeps the business engine humming, making it even easier to generate faster results.

Effortless Growth

Without growth, every business venture would eventually die…

Every business venture is born like a baby and needs to be fed and nurtured to succeed…

The tools for nurturing a business come in various forms and shapes; they include good leadership structure, clear business model, working operational structures, business assets, products and services, resources and funds, and a working marketing plan that guarantees revenue generation.

Without these tools working synergistically, growth would be a mirage for any business and that's a clear sign of business failure.

Creating an atmosphere for synergy both within the internal and external business environments, for example, finding trustable suppliers, gaining market share and acceptability for your products, building a strong customer base, building strong partnerships, and adopting technology, will make your business to have few hoops to jump and be able to grow effortlessly.

Take Advantage of Existing Business Structures

Big corporations have often taken advantage of the power of synergy to grow and exert their dominance within and outside their industry by simply buying existing businesses and knocking competition out of the way.

When they do this through mergers or acquisitions, they simply take advantage of these old businesses' existing structures, and instead of building from scratch, they take what already works and remodels it to fit their bigger business goals.

This is one big advantage of synergy which works for big companies with deep pockets, but how does this apply to small business owners and entrepreneurs, ambitious but with very shallow or even no pockets at all?

The answer is what we will be talking about in-depth in the next chapter.

Rapid Expansion

Businesses that strategically exploit business synergy often grow and expand rapidly…

One of the old models by which many big corporations that exist today grew and expanded into new geographic territories both locally and internationally was through franchising.

Franchising is a form of synergy where a business brand grants an individual or a group the license to make or market their goods or services in a given territory.

This model allows these brands to take advantage of the local knowledge of the franchise partners in the new territory to open new markets, grow and extend their brand name at no extra cost.

Coca-Cola, Pepsi, McDonald, KFC, are all global franchises today because of the synergistic power of franchising.

Cutting Cost

Creating business synergies can help companies and business owners lower the cost of running or marketing their businesses in so many ways.

Large companies acquire small ones and build off of their existing products without the need to start from ground zero to build and test new products, which saves them millions of dollars in testing ideas that may not work.

Small business owners can form Joint Venture partnerships with more experienced entrepreneurs and tap into the knowledge base of the more experienced partners to create and launch products.

This guarantees more safety and gives the small business more chances of success. We will talk about this even more in chapter four.

Chapter 3

How to Create Profitable Business Synergies

We have talked about business synergy, what it is, and the advantages and benefits of creating synergies within the internal business environment, and outside of it.

Right now, it's time to zoom in on how you can take advantage of business synergy to grow your business and revenue as a small business.

What I want to do is to help you see that synergy is for everyone, not just the corporate deep-pocket big boys.

There's always an opportunity for profitable synergy for every business.

All it takes to see the abounding opportunities is, first of all, to look within and identify the key needle-movers in your business.

Understanding what moves the needle for your business is the lock you have to pick first, and when you unlock this, every other thing kind of begins to fit in.

Let's talk about what these needle-movers are.

Your Business Model and Business Strategy

A business model is a description of how your business makes money.

Your business strategy helps you answer three questions.

- What is our product or service and what does it take to make it?

- How do we sell the product (marketing, sales, distribution, service delivery)?

- How much do we sell it (pricing strategy, payment methods, etc.)?

Answering these questions clearly and succinctly will help you plan and structure your business properly.

It will help you begin to see the areas of the business where you will need help... and these are the areas where you will have to form synergistic partnerships to achieve results faster.

With a clear business model and structure, it becomes easier to set target goals and get them scored by your team because everyone knows what is required, and what needs to be done.

Knowing your business model can help to establish internal synergy for your business.

Know Your Marketing Audience Inside-out

Oftentimes entrepreneurs get so engrossed and obsessed with their products and how wonderful it is that they completely lose sight of the end-user.

They forget to consider that their customers don't really care about their product's awesome features and design.

What the customers want is a solution to their problems, and it is your duty as an entrepreneur to turn all the nice features into tangible benefits and a solution to your customer's problem.

This is why knowing your marketing audience inside out is very important.

What are their challenges and problems that your product solves?

Where do they hang out or converge, both offline and online?

What solutions are they looking for?

What TV shows or YouTube channels do they watch?

What podcasts do they listen to?

What blogs do they visit and read?

Who do they follow on social media?

Who are the top influencers and thought leaders in your industry your audience follows and listens to?

These are some of the most important questions you need to provide answers to as you research your target market…

Even more important is the last question. It can tremendously help you to rapidly build synergy and grow your business at a lower cost…

And that's what we will be talking about next.

Thinking Collaboration over Competition

In his best-selling book Traffic Secrets, award-winning entrepreneur Russell Brunson talked about how thinking collaboration over competition helped him to build multi-million-dollar businesses and sold millions of copies of his books.

Russell Brunson is the founder of ClickFunnel, a multimillion-dollar Software as a Service (SaaS) company he co-founded and built from scratch without any venture capitalist investment.

Russell was able to achieve this because he mastered the secret of business synergy and leverage

In his book, Traffic Secrets, Russell distilled his methods into the concept of the dream 100.

The Dream 100

Russell defined the dream 100 as the list of 100 persons who currently control your dream customers, in other words, your dream 100 is a list that contains the top 100 influencers and thought-leaders in your industry whom your dream customers follow, trust, and consume their content.

The idea is that if you can build a relationship with one of this dream 100, and get a yes to promote your business with them, that could turn into hundreds or thousands of new customers in one fell swoop.

So, by focusing on identifying your dream 100 and working hard to build a synergistic relationship with them, you can easily penetrate their audience and market and start generating more revenue without blowing your marketing budget. This way you can build synergy with established industry big dogs and grow your business exponentially.

How to Establish Your Dream 100

It's not difficult finding the industry thought leaders that fall into your dream 100, what's difficult is building an important relationship with them.

To establish your dream 100, you will need to look back at your business model and your target market.

Once you know how your business makes money and who exactly your customer is...

Then the one question whose answer will point you to your dream 100 is this:

Who are the established thought leaders that my potential customers follow, buy their products, or consume their content?

A quick Google search will point you to your list.

And the beautiful thing about searching and digging out this list is that once you know one thought-leader or influencer, you can easily find others like him or her by simply searching and following them on social media and following the auto-suggested pages of people like your target thought leader.

After establishing your dream 100, then the next thing on the list will be to start making moves to connect and build a relationship with them.

There are so many tactics you can use to do this…

- You can ask for a recommendation through your existing network

- You can sign up for their programs, buy their products, or attend events they host, where you can network and get the chance to meet.

☐ You can mail them a handwritten postcard appreciating them for what they do and working it up from there.

☐ If you have a product, you can ship it to them and ask them to test it out.

The idea is to go the extra mile to start a conversation that leads to building a strong relationship that can spill over into a partnership and business synergy.

Chapter 4

Modern Ways Small Businesses and Entrepreneurs Build Profitable Synergies

#1. Affiliate Marketing

Affiliate marketing is both a business synergy and a business model.

Powered by the internet, affiliate marketing is one of the quickest ways savvy entrepreneurs and brands are using to gain market share, grow their business, and generate more revenue.

Affiliate marketing allows businesses to penetrate new marketing audiences by leveraging internet content publishers to promote their products to their large followership and email lists in exchange for sales commissions.

The beauty of affiliate marketing is that it can drastically reduce your business's marketing budget and ad costs.

Here are some of the popular affiliate networks entrepreneurs are taking advantage of.

- ClickBank
- WarriorPlus
- JVZoo
- Digistore24
- Etc.

All you have to do is be willing to share profits with your army of affiliates.

The Affiliate marketing model has made many entrepreneurs very rich and it's booming, with both old and new affiliate networks growing to serve the market.

#2. Joint Ventures

JVs as they are called are helping small business owners and entrepreneurs grow and generate more revenues.

A joint venture is a business arrangement where two businesses, business owners, or entrepreneurs, partner to share expertise resources and achieve a common profitable business goal.

By sharing expertise and resources joint ventures reduce costs and shrink the business cycle. It becomes easier to achieve set business goals.

If you are looking to enter into a joint venture, it is prudent to look for a brand that possesses what your business currently lacks; it can be resources, assets, or expertise, and then approach them for a JV partnership and then share profits.

Entering a joint venture with another entrepreneur or business in the same capacity as yours is a bad idea.

#3. Task Outsourcing

Outsourcing is another way entrepreneurs are establishing synergy for their businesses by taking advantage of freelance workplaces like Upwork and Fiverr.

Instead of hiring full-time skills and dealing with payroll, entrepreneurs are shrinking the cost of running their businesses by outsourcing business tasks to experienced freelancers which leaves them the time to focus on the major needle-movers of their business.

30

Conclusion

As you have seen, business synergy is not just for big corporations, as an entrepreneur and small business owner, there are many ways you can take advantage of synergy to grow your business to profitability.

We have looked at many of them in this book, and now I hope you can see the many synergy opportunities staring at you.

Now, you can begin to take advantage of them to propel your business growth for good.